PAUL
writes
(a letter)

Chris Raschka

Eerdmans Books for Young Readers

Grand Rapids, Michigan

for Mary

Eerdmans Books for Young Readers, an imprint of Wm. B. Eerdmans Publishing Co. • 2140 Oak Industrial Dr. NE Grand Rapids, Michigan 49505
ISBN 978-0-8028-5494-0 • A catalog record of this book is available from the Library of Congress • Illustrations created with watercolor.

A couple thousand years ago, there lived a man named Paul. He was a faithful and learned man who, in the middle of his life, began to believe in the story of the life and teachings of Jesus. He traveled all over the world he knew, which was the Roman Empire, to talk about his new way of thinking. During his travels, he wrote letters to the people he had seen or would see soon.

Remember: love your neighbor as much as you love yourselves.

Please greet my friend Priscilla for me.

Also my friend Phoebe is on her way to see you.

Grace be with you. PAUL

16:1-3

There is faith. There is hope. There is caring for others. The greatest is caring for others.

I'm planning a trip to see you this winter on my way to Macedonia. Priscilla says hello. Be strong. PAUL

16:13, 16:19

My earlier letter upset you. Good!
Sometimes we need to be upset.
I wrote as I did because I care about you.

My words can be with you even as a part of me.

I would like to visit you again for a third time, and I hope not to be a burden.
Peace, PAUL

10:11, 12:14, 13:11

Dear Friends in Galatia, Only remember one thing: love others just the way you love yourselves.

GAL 5:14, 6:7-10, 6:17

You reap what you sow. If you begin something out of badness, badness will grow. If you begin something out of goodness, goodness will grow. Please don't bother me if you don't like this letter. PAUL

Make good things with your hands.

Children, obey your parents.

Parents, don't wind up your children.

My friend Tychicus is coming to you and will tell you more about me.

Be tenderhearted. PAUL

Dear Friends in Philippi,
I am with Timothy
and we send
you peace.

PHIL 1:1-2, 4:8, 4:12, 4:21

Whatever is true, whatever is honest, whatever is just, whatever is pure, whatever ♣ is lovely, whatever you have heard good things about, these are the things you should muse on.
I have learned no matter how things are with me, good or bad, I can be happy.
Greetings from all my friends, PAUL

Dear Friends in Colossae, Be patient with one another.

COL 3:12-14, 3:23, 4:14,

When you get dressed, put on **Kindness.**

Clothe yourselves in **love.** Whatever you do, do it **heartily.**

Grace be with you. **PAUL**

Luke, the doctor, and **Demas** say hello.

4:18

Work with your own hands. Comfort the timid. Help the weak.

please share this letter. PAUL

My Friends in
Thessalonica,

II THESS 1:2, 3:11-12, 3:16

Now I hear some of you are busybodies.

Please stop that and quietly get back to your own work.

Peace, Paul

Be good and therefore happy.

If you love money, it will ruin you. Fight the good fight. Grace be with you. PAUL.

6:12, 6:21

Dear Timothy, Your good faith is true like your grandmother's and your mother's too.

Don't be ashamed of what you believe in. It has been difficult for me too, and now I am a prisoner in Rome.

II TIM 1:5-6, 1:8, 4:7,

Dear Philemon and Apphia and Archippus, You refresh the very hearts of the saints.

PHLM 1:1-2, 1:7, 1:24

HEB 11:1, 13:23-25

At the end of his time
as a prisoner,

Paul
was killed
by his jailers with a
sword.

His symbols in art
are a sword
and a book.

Also, one more thing: some biblical
scholars doubt that Paul wrote Hebrews.
Who did? We don't know who did for
certain. I've chosen the parts that
sound like Paul to me.

And believe me, or believe me not, this one man, Paul, by writing letters to his friends, changed the world.

That is why some people call him Saint Paul.